HUMANIMAL

Incredible Ways Animals Are Just Like Us!

BY
CHRISTOPHER LLOYD

ILLUSTRATED BY
MARK RUFFLE

What on Earth Books

To Flossie and Millie, who have made our family experience humanimal in far more ways than words can say.

CONTENTS

Irene Pepperberg with Alex

FOREWORD

All over the world and for hundreds of thousands of years, the ancestors of today's indigenous people lived close to wild animals. They passed along cultural traditions of respect for animals as the equals or sometimes the superiors of humans.

As time passed, many humans left their homes in the wild and gathered together in cities and towns. Seeing less of wild animals changed our ways of thinking about them. We began to believe that humans were better, smarter, more powerful and more important than the animals around us. Look at us, we said to one another, we have figured out how to farm the land and raise the few animals we like to eat. We communicate using language. We invent things. We live in big cities. We build giant buildings. We organise our societies. Some of us even vote to decide what to do. Plus on top of all of that, we are fantastic problem solvers, we are aware of ourselves as individuals and we feel deep emotions. All of those things make us special.

Scientists agreed. They came up with a simple definition of humans that went like this: humans are tool makers. Making and using tools sets us apart from the rest of the animal world.

Things went along that way for a while. Then, in the middle of the 1900s, something big changed. A small number of scientists started doing something that scientists hadn't done before. They went out into the wild and watched animals. And they didn't watch for a few hours or a few days the way tourists and hunters did. They watched for many years, taking notes and photos and videos so they could remember what they had seen and share their observations with the world. And one of their first discoveries changed everything. Jane Goodall, working in Tanzania, saw chimpanzees making and using tools. Yikes! Our definition of humans was out the window.

Since then, thousands of scientists have observed a huge range of animals in the wild, from chimpanzees to whales to bees. And others have worked with captive animals or measured animal brain chemistry or analysed animal DNA to learn even more.

So here's the upshot: it turns out that the respect for animals that is so important in indigenous traditions makes very good sense. Most of our ideas about humans as the best, smartest, deepest-feeling creatures ever? Wrong, or at least mostly. There are some things humans do that animals don't. So far, no other animal has flown to the moon, for example. But in many other ways, animals are astonishingly like humans.

Animals are so much like us that as I wrote this book I kept thinking that we need a new word, one that helps us understand how much we have in common. So I made one up and used it as the title. I hope once you've read the book, you'll agree ... we're all Humanimal!

Christopher Lloyd
May 2019

COMMUNITY

Humans live in families and communities of every shape and size. We work together, too. We build buildings, raise crops and animals and make decisions together about what needs to be done when. We support one another, lending our special strengths to help the whole group succeed. And we show off what we do best.

Then, when the work is done (and sometimes when it isn't), we play together. Sometimes we play games like football or rugby, but we're often just as happy playing tag or rolling down a snowy hill.

It turns out that none of this makes us very special. Scientists working around the world have found animals working in teams, farming and building towers complete with climate control. Some animals go to great lengths to show off for others. And it even looks as if some play for the pure joy of it.

In the Spring, Mexican free-tailed bat communities split into groups. The adult males create several small all-male groups for the season. The adult females and their babies stay together in one huge group. These nursery groups can be gigantic. The biggest, in Bracken Cave in Texas, USA, has up to 20 million bats. The babies keep themselves safely on the cave walls by using their feet and thumbs to cling to the walls and one another.

TEAMWORK

Humans work together all the time. And it's a pretty tricky business. Even just deciding what film to see or where to go shopping at the weekend can be a big challenge for a family or group of friends.

Honeybees are brilliant at working together. One way they do it is by sharing information – when gathering food, for example. Picture this: one bee finds a particularly good patch of flowers with plenty of nectar and pollen to eat. It flies back to the hive to let all the other bees know where they can find this yummy food. But how does the bee explain? An Austrian scientist called Karl von Frisch discovered the answer.

Von Frisch figured out that bees communicate through dancing. A bee that has just found food does a waggling dance in front of the other bees. The dance is just like talking, only with movements instead of words.

The bee shows where the food is located through the direction of their waggle. If it dances towards the top of the hive, that means the other bees should fly towards the sun to find the food. So whatever angle it dances away from the top of the hive shows where the food is located in

Bees gather around a bee who is dancing to show the location of a new source of food.

relation to the sun. The bee also lets the other bees smell the nectar on them, so they know the type of flower they have found. Scientists don't know for sure, but it looks as if a longer, repetitive dance means more food.

Von Frisch's student, Martin Lindauer, realised something even more amazing. Bees vote! Every spring, healthy honeybee hives that have become crowded divide in two. A daughter queen stays at the old nest with half of the bees. The rest of the bees start a new hive with the old queen. Before they can move, though, the bees have to figure out where to build the new hive.

This is how they do it. Firstly, scout bees fly out to look for a prime location. Each one returns to the group and reports its findings by dancing. The other bees watch the scouts dance and then head out to check out the options. They return to the hive and vote for their favourite site by dancing the same dance as the bee that originally found it. The most popular place gets the most bees dancing, and that's where the bees will set up their new hive.

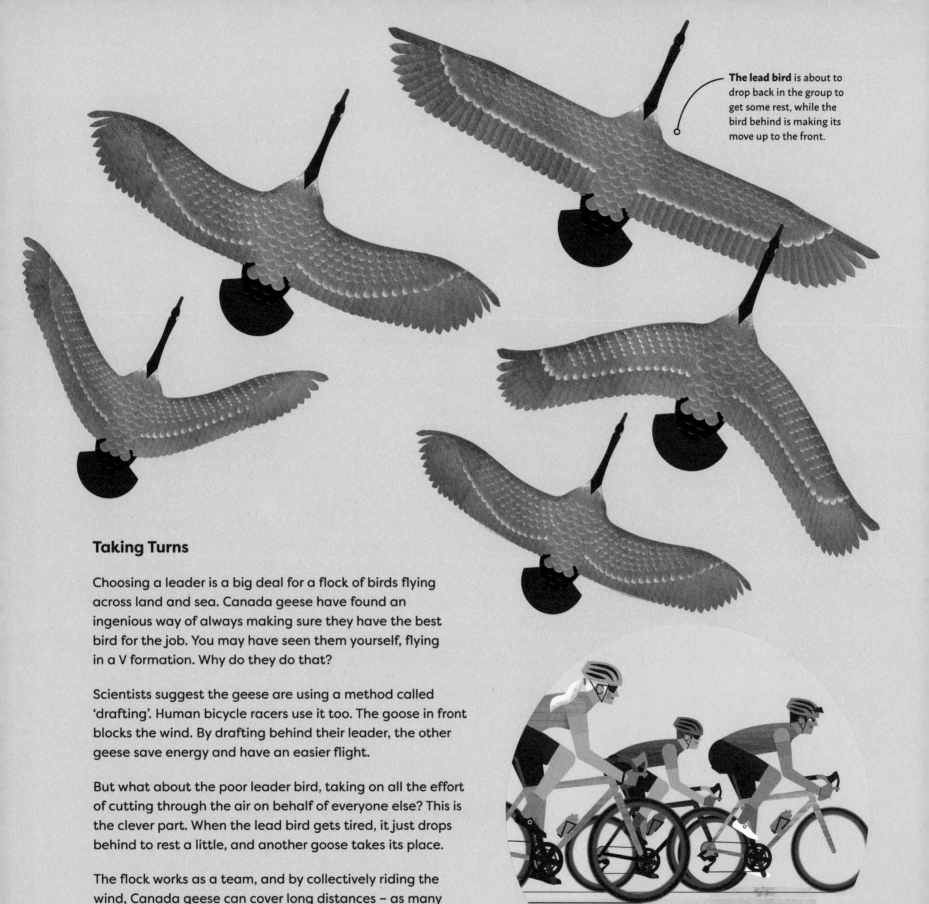

The lead bird is about to drop back in the group to get some rest, while the bird behind is making its move up to the front.

Taking Turns

Choosing a leader is a big deal for a flock of birds flying across land and sea. Canada geese have found an ingenious way of always making sure they have the best bird for the job. You may have seen them yourself, flying in a V formation. Why do they do that?

Scientists suggest the geese are using a method called 'drafting'. Human bicycle racers use it too. The goose in front blocks the wind. By drafting behind their leader, the other geese save energy and have an easier flight.

But what about the poor leader bird, taking on all the effort of cutting through the air on behalf of everyone else? This is the clever part. When the lead bird gets tired, it just drops behind to rest a little, and another goose takes its place.

The flock works as a team, and by collectively riding the wind, Canada geese can cover long distances – as many as 2,400 kilometres in twenty-four hours. That's equivalent to travelling from London in the UK to Athens in Greece in a day – a feat that would be quite impossible for a goose on its own.

Cyclists at the front of a race fight the full force of the wind. They take turns to drop behind the leader, where they are more sheltered and use less energy.

FARMING

Imagine alien researchers arrive from outer space and see the Earth for the first time. What do you think they'd write in their log book? I'd guess the fact that a third of the world's land is used to raise plants and animals as food for one species (us!) would be high on their list. But if those aliens did their research properly, they'd realise that humans aren't the world's only farmers. For a start, they'd just need to look at ants.

Leafcutter ants have been farming for at least sixty million years. They use their jaws to cut through leaves and then carry pieces back to their nests – no easy task as the leaves are huge compared with their tiny body size. The ants crush the leaves and use them to feed a fungus they grow for food. As the white fluffy fungus matures, it gives off spores (which are kind of like seeds). The ants give the spores more leaves, and the spores grow into more fungus.

Like human farmers, ants take care of their gardens. They weed out other kinds of fungus so there's plenty of room for the kind they like to eat. They even mix their own poo into the mashed-up bits of leaves to make them more nutritious for the fungus, just as human farmers use manure to produce better crops. In return for all this hard work, the ants are rewarded with a steady supply of food.

Leafcutter ants make sure that their gardens are free of disease. They rub a bacteria that lives on their bodies onto the fungus, which helps to protect it from pests.

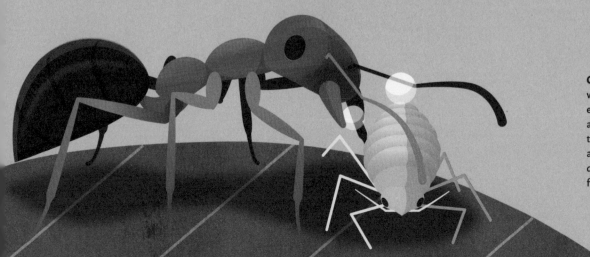

Other types of ants farm their own food, too. Just the way humans keep cows for milk, big-headed ants raise even smaller bugs called aphids. They make sure the aphids always have plenty of food to eat. Then, when the ants are hungry, they stroke the aphids with their antennae. This causes the aphids to produce a sugary drink known as honeydew, a delicious and nutritious food for the ants.

Fish Farmers

Dive deep and you'll find animals farming in the sea, too. In 2002, a group of Japanese scientists including Hiroki Hata discovered dusky farmerfish, a species of damselfish, acting like human farmers.

Dusky farmerfish live in tropical coral reefs. They are fussy eaters and prefer a certain seaweed called *Polysiphonia*. To make sure they always have plenty of this nutritious food, they remove other types of seaweed from where *Polysiphonia* grows, just the way humans weed their vegetable gardens.

Parrotfish

Dusky farmerfish

The relationship between damselfish and *Polysiphonia* is called mutualism. This is when two different types of living things help each other survive.

Polysiphonia

Convict surgeonfish

12

Rabbitfish

Dusky farmerfish chase away other animals looking to eat their crops, just as human farmers might scare off rabbits or birds from their fields. Invaders might include sea urchins, parrotfish, convict surgeonfish and rabbitfish.

Sea urchin

CITY LIVING

There's a real buzz about living in a city. Have you ever sat on a bench and just watched people going about their busy lives? Everyone is doing different things. They shop, they eat, they work, they clean. Well it turns out that busy living isn't unique to New York, London or Beijing. Can you think of any other creatures that buzz and live in giant swarms? Insects including bees, wasps, ants and termites created the world's first giant cities millions of years before humans appeared.

Termites are famous for their mounds, which can house as many as a million termites. Inside there are separate areas for growing and storing food, gardens with edible fungus grown by worker termites, nurseries for baby termites and a royal chamber for the queen. A termite city can stretch more than five metres high. That's taller than a double-decker bus!

The central chimney is surrounded by a maze of tunnels that let fresh air in and stale air out. This helps with climate control and ventilation.

Some chambers of the termite mound contain food (like wood and grass) stored by worker termites. Others are gardens, where termites grow fungus to help them extract nutrients from their food.

Workers repair a damaged mound.

The towering mound is made of soil, termite saliva and dung. It helps to protect the colony.

Just as houses have heating and air conditioning, the chimney and tunnels of the mound keep the termites moist and cool. This is super important in the dry African savannah where they live.

Worker termites do all of the work in the nest. One group are the engineers. They build the mound using dirt and their own saliva and dung. This is very similar to an old-fashioned human building method using pieces of wood (called wattle) and a mixture of dirt and cow dung (known as daub). But no wattle and daub structure we know of is as complex as a termite mound!

Termite engineers also fix the mound if any part of it gets damaged. Most termite mounds take years to build from scratch. But termites have been known to rebuild a badly damaged mound in as few as three months.

The termites live below ground in chambers within a large oval nest.

The queen is a huge termite. Her role is to lay eggs that hatch into baby termites, making sure the colony has plenty of workers. She lives in a special room and is looked after by a group of worker termites.

COMMUNITY

HAVING FUN

I am lucky enough to live with two dogs, Flossie and Millie. For ten years, Flossie was the only dog in our house. She went on walks with us and sat on our laps. But she didn't run around much and she never barked. Plus, when she met other dogs she usually shied away. So we were all a bit nervous when we first introduced Flossie to our new puppy, Millie. Would they get along? Would Flossie be jealous?

To our amazement, Flossie liked Millie! And not only that, she stopped being so quiet and shy. Now, every day, just after dinner, it's playtime. Flossie and Millie roar around the house playing hide-and-seek. Flossie barks to tease Millie out of her hiding places, and then they race around some more. It seems so obvious that Flossie and Millie are having fun!

Just like dogs, people like to play, too! Scientists have discovered an important chemical that is produced by our brains when we're happy. It is called dopamine. And when people are doing something just for the pure fun of it, their brains release dopamine. Some recent research suggests that when rats play, their brains also release dopamine. Experts can now see that what happens in rat and human brains may be very similar. As to why rats play? Because it's fun, of course! People, dogs, rats and even some birds all play for fun – it's humanimal.

Ravens have been spotted rolling down snowy hills and then climbing back up and doing it again. Crows do this sort of thing too. Are they playing? That's a pretty good explanation. Just like people, these birds seem to roll downhill simply for the fun of it.

SHOWING OFF

Some people play incredible guitar solos. Others charge around a sports field, skilfully dribbling a football and scoring goals. What makes you stand out from the crowd? Maybe it's break dancing or painting portraits or wearing the latest styles?

Music, sport, art and fashion are all examples of how people show off to one another. Showing off is such a natural part of our everyday lives that it's tempting to think only humans do it. After all, when's the last time you saw a dog play the piano? Or a bird ride a bike? But many other animals are instinctive show-offs too.

Meet one of nature's finest artists. The Vogelkop bowerbird lives on the tropical island of New Guinea, off the north coast of Australia. The male bird collects objects and carefully spreads them out on the forest floor like a fine Persian carpet. Behind this base, it builds a bower: a spiral of twigs carefully woven around a small young tree. The bower and display of objects is the male's way of showing off to females.

Birds are not the only animals that show off to attract mates. Male pufferfish create gorgeous two-metre-wide sand nests to impress female pufferfish. It takes them more than ten days of careful work.

The bowerbird collects objects like fruits, flowers, stones, acorns and snail shells to make a colourful display.

FEELINGS

If you have a dog, does it really love you? Or does it just act like it loves you when it wants a treat? Scientists have struggled with questions like these, but they are starting to find the answers.

Nerves in fish turn out to be the same as those in other creatures with backbones, including dogs and humans. Scientists have also found that if a fish panics, the same drugs that make humans calmer also help the fish. Anger, pain, joy, fear and grief are likely to be similar in humans and other animals, too. It looks as if feelings might be humanimal.

A polar bear mum takes care of her cub for two or three years. Mother and baby play together, rolling around in the snow. Mum keeps her cub close, making a clacking sound to call it back to her side. She also protects her cub from other polar bears and teaches it how to hunt, so it can fend for itself when it is old enough. Do the mum and cub love each other? It looks as if they do.

LOVE

We humans love a lot of people in a lot of different ways. We love our families, our friends and our partners. But do animals do the same? It certainly looks like it.

Bonobos are great apes closely related to humans. In 2011, a group of researchers from Japan and the Democratic Republic of the Congo were tracking a gang of about twenty bonobos. One day, the group was looking for fruit in a swampy area. One of them, a male the researchers called Malusu, got his hand caught in a metal trap. Malusu broke the small tree the trap was attached to. Then another member of his group unwound the vines that held the broken tree to the trap, tried to remove the trap from Malusu's hand, and licked his wounds. But as Malusu started moving around, the trap got stuck in vines again.

When evening came, the bonobos returned to the safety of the dry forest where they slept. They left Malusu behind, still tangled in vines. But in the morning, the same group hiked back more than a mile to where they had left their friend. They found that Malusu had freed himself and moved on. The group's return is a clear example of animals caring for friends, just the way humans do.

Bonobo love isn't just for friends, either. Researchers in North Carolina, USA, have shown that bonobos will share food with others, even when they have never met before.

Macaroni penguins, who can be found in South America and in Antarctica, get excited when they see their mate. They swing their bright yellow-crested heads and squawk at each other in what is known as an 'ecstatic display'.

Blue footed boobies are goose-sized sea birds that live off the western coasts of Central and South America. They have brown speckled heads and big blue webbed feet. When a male and female booby decide to team up, the couple often stays together for life. And as in many human families, male and female blue-footed boobies share the job of raising their young. But that's not all. The baby boobies take care of one another. Scientists have found that when there is a brief shortage in food, stronger chicks let the weaker siblings get a fair share.

AGGRESSION

When was the last time you got really angry and yelled at someone? Maybe they broke something you really loved. Or maybe they said something horrible. Even though we try to control our tempers, anger and aggression are completely natural. Animals get aggressive, too.

Canadian zoologist Anne Innis Dagg is a world expert on giraffes and one of the very first scientists to spend years watching animals in the wild. She observed that male giraffes can battle for the right to mate with females. They throw their long, heavy necks and heads against one other with all their strength. Giraffe necks can stretch up to 1.8 metres long and weigh 270 kilograms. While these contests can be very fierce, the giraffes are rarely seriously hurt. The weaker giraffe usually gives up before that can happen.

You know how some people's faces turn red when they're angry? Well, a few years ago, Alaskan scientist David Scheel and his research team found that octopuses turn a different colour when they're aggressive, too!

Be careful if you see an angry cat. You can tell if a cat is cross because it holds out its tail stiff and long, and its entire body turns rigid. Sometimes it hisses or growls and pulls its body upwards to look as big as possible.

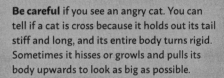

Alex was an African grey parrot who knew how to use more than a hundred English words. American scientist Irene Pepperberg noted that when Alex was expecting a treat of a cashew nut but was given a bird pellet instead, he would puff up his feathers and clearly state 'Wanna nut!'

When fruit flies get angry they puff up their wings as high as they can to look more threatening to rival flies.

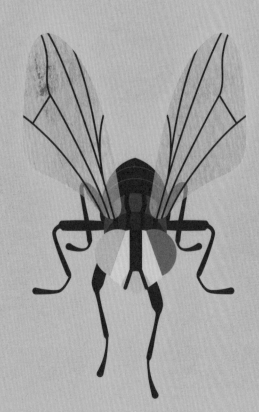

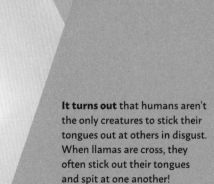

It turns out that humans aren't the only creatures to stick their tongues out at others in disgust. When llamas are cross, they often stick out their tongues and spit at one another!

GRIEF

One of the most powerful feelings of all is the sadness and loss when someone we care about dies. But is the same true for animals? Do cats feel terribly sad when a family member dies? Do fish miss their departed friends? It looks as if the answer might be at least partly yes.

A team of scientists from the University of Pennsylvania, led by Anne Engh, studied chacma baboons in the Okavango Delta in Botswana to better understand the monkeys' emotions. We know that in humans, different chemicals released by the body are related to different feelings. So the scientists are looking at which chemicals are being released by the baboons. They do this by looking at the chemicals found in female baboons' poo.

Sometimes a close friend or family member of one of these baboons is killed by a predator, such as a crocodile or lion. When that happens, the surviving baboon releases a chemical called cortisol. It's the same one humans release at times of great stress. Other monkeys in the troop stroke and groom the sad baboon to help it feel better.

This suggests that animals grieve, just as humans do. For a chacma baboon, the grieving period seems to last about a month. After that, its cortisol levels return to normal.

Grieving Whales

Orcas, also known as killer whales, live in family groups called pods. They hunt, play and relax together. One orca mother, known as Tahlequah, lives in the waters off the Pacific coast of Canada and the USA. In July 2018, Tahlequah's baby died. At sunset that day, a resident of San Juan Island in Washington State saw five or six female orcas swimming in a tight circle for two hours, lit up by a moonbeam. After this, Tahlequah carried her dead calf for seventeen days before finally letting it go.

Was the swimming circle a sort of funeral for the baby? Did Tahlequah carry her baby for so long because she didn't want to accept its death? We don't know for sure. Scientists have discovered that some whales, including orcas, have spindle cells in their brains. These same cells are what allow humans to process feelings. So it is certainly possible that this orca behaviour is a sign that they feel grief.

Mourning Elephants

When Shifra Goldenberg was studying at Colorado State University, she witnessed the final days of an old African elephant that died surrounded by her family. Several weeks later, Shifra returned and saw the other elephants inspecting her bones. Were they grieving, as humans do? Experts don't know. But their keen interest in the remains may be one way these magnificent creatures understand and deal with the loss.

FEELINGS

INTELLIGENCE

Are you good at solving problems? Writing stories? Doing sums in your head? Some people are clever at some things and other people are clever at other things. But, when it comes down to it, most people are good enough learners, adapters and problem solvers to survive in our rapidly changing world. That's what scientists call intelligence.

Other animals have intelligence, too. Humans can recognise themselves in the mirror – but so can dolphins and orangutans. Humans have amazing communication skills, but so do whales and chickens. Humans solve puzzles and use tools, but so do slime moulds and chimpanzees. Humans lie and deceive others, but so do cuckoos and butterflies. Intelligence is yet another humanimal thing.

Female cuckoos secretly lay eggs in other birds' nests. Why on earth would they do this? The idea is to trick another bird (often a reed warbler) into taking care of the baby cuckoo egg, along with its own. But it gets worse. As soon as the baby cuckoo hatches, it pushes the warbler eggs out of the nest. The adult reed warblers end up losing their own chicks and raising the cuckoo chick instead.

SELF-AWARENESS

Zoos are wonderful places to observe lots of different animals.
On a sunny summer's day in 1838, the famous British scientist Charles
Darwin visited London Zoo. One creature caught his eye. It was an
orangutan – a type of great ape – named Jenny. Darwin noticed that
when Jenny looked at herself in a mirror, she seemed surprised.

Did she know she was looking at herself, he thought? Or did
she think she was looking at another orangutan? It was impossible
to be sure.

More than 100 years later, an American psychologist named Gordon
Gallup Jr. used mirrors to test whether other creatures could recognise
themselves. The idea was simple. Place a mark on an animal's face.

Then give the animal a mirror. If it touched the mark on its face, that would show it knew that the animal in the mirror was itself!

Gallup tested four chimpanzees. All four chimps passed the mirror test with flying colours. Scientists have found strong evidence that orangutans can also recognise themselves, and some think that all the great apes, elephants, dolphins, orcas, magpies, and even ants might be able to as well.

Of course, not all creatures use sight as their primary sense. Some use smell or sound. Today, researchers are working on ways to help us understand how those creatures understand themselves and how this may help animals, including humans, connect with others in their social groups.

In 2006, Joshua Plotnik, a student at Emory University, USA, tested Asian elephants at the Bronx Zoo in New York City. One of the elephants was named Happy. When she looked in a mirror, she used her long trunk to touch a white mark that Plotnik had painted on her head. It's clear that she knew she was looking at herself.

When bottlenose dolphins see themselves in a mirror, they stick out their tongues and make strange movements, as if checking to see, 'is this really me?'.

LANGUAGE

If you ask someone in the street what they think is the biggest difference between humans and animals, chances are they may say that we talk and they don't. But it turns out that's just not true.

Humpback whales are famous for singing songs, and baleen whales can make their sounds heard across vast distances underwater. A team of researchers including Magnus Wahlberg and Cláudia Oliveira studied the sounds of sperm whales in the Atlantic Ocean. What they found was that sperm whales seem to communicate with each other in a way that might be a bit like two people talking together.

During their research, the scientists recorded twenty-one different whale messages. Like Morse code, the messages are made up of a series of tapping sounds. For example, one message had four long taps followed by two short ones. So far, no one has deciphered the messages, but the researchers have theories. They think they may identify each whale in a group, or signal whether a whale is about to dive or come to the surface. Perhaps they are announcing that food has been found, or maybe mothers are calling to their young.

Clever Chickens

You might think that chickens aren't too clever. But scientists believe that they are intelligent creatures, with smart ways of communicating with each other.

Researchers have spent years listening to chickens to try and find patterns in the sounds they make. Sure enough, chickens seem to use at least twenty-four vocalisations (or sounds) that mean particular things.

Gail Damerow, from Tennessee, USA, has written many books on raising chickens, including a chicken encyclopedia. She says: 'Repeated sharp, loud tweets mean, "I am so miserable" probably because they are too hot, cold or hungry. A loud sharp repeated trill sound means, "Don't hurt me", whereas short low-pitched repetitive clucks mean, "Stay close".'

PEEP, PEEP, PEEP
Mummy, where are you?

COOO
Yum!

TUCK TUCK TUCK
Ooh, I can see some tasty food

CUH CAAAH, CUH CAAAH, CUH CAAH
Watch out, there's a hawk nearby!

CLUCK CLUCK CLUCK
Stay close

HISSSSS
Get away from my eggs!

DECEPTION

Many animals are brilliant at deception. In fact, the better some animals are at outsmarting others, the more successful they become – because it helps them survive.

The fork-tailed drongo is an African songbird. It lives alongside meerkats, mammals that often gather in large groups. Meerkats eat insects. Drongos like insects, too, and have clever ways of stealing them from the meerkats.

When an eagle flies overhead hunting for meerkats, the drongo makes a piercing warning call. The meerkats run into the safety of their underground burrows. After this works a few times, the meerkats learn to trust the drongo's warning. The next time the drongo sees the meerkats dining on tasty-looking insects, it makes its alarm sound, even though there are no eagles around. The meerkats leave their food and flee, fearing for their lives. The drongo dives in and gobbles up what's left of the meerkats' meal.

Sometimes, the sneaky drongo will even copy the warning sound of the meerkats themselves. It's not just meerkats that fall for these tricks. Scientists think drongos have a toolkit of around fifty alarm calls, so they can deceive other animals, too. In fact, drongos get a good portion of their food by stealing it from other creatures.

African monarch caterpillars feed on the toxic milkweed plant. Then, when they become butterflies, they are poisonous to predators. The bright patterns on their wings warn other creatures that eating the butterfly will make them sick. The diadem, another butterfly, is not at all poisonous. Instead, it simply shares the monarch's colouring, which fools predators into keeping away.

The mimic octopus was first identified in Indonesia in 1998. It changes its shape and colour as well as the pattern and texture of its skin to look like at least fifteen other animals. When it is in shallow sandy river bottoms, it uses drab brown colours to blend in with its surroundings. When it is in open water, it looks like a poisonous flatfish or sea snake to protect itself from predators.

PUZZLE SOLVING

Slime mould can be found growing on rotting trees in damp woodland. Not a likely place, you might think, to find intelligence. But this humble creature can actually learn and solve problems.

There are a lot of kinds of slime mould. One type is *Physarum polycephalum*. Its name means 'many-headed slime', but it doesn't have any heads at all, or any nerves or brain. Instead it is one giant cell with the ability to push out its body in lots of different directions to look for food.

But this slime can do much more. Scientists have shown that it can make decisions, recognise where it has been, map territory and move with intention, all meaning that it is able to find the best way from point A to point B.

A team headed by Toshiyuki Nakagaki in Japan made a map of the city of Tokyo and placed a porridge oat flake at each of the busiest places in the city. Then they put a blob of slime at the centre of the map. The slime spread out, figured out the quickest ways between oat flakes (a yummy food for slime), and placed most of its body on the best routes. In the end, it looked very much like the Tokyo subway system, which humans had spent years designing to be the most efficient possible way to travel around the city.

At the same time, UK researchers proposed to use slime mould to help plan transport systems. Andrew Adamatzky in Bristol has used slime to figure out which road systems in the world already work well and which could use some improvements. Slime can also handle unexpected problems. When a researcher puts a little salt (which is poisonous to slime) where an obstacle would be on the map, the slime comes up with the best way around it.

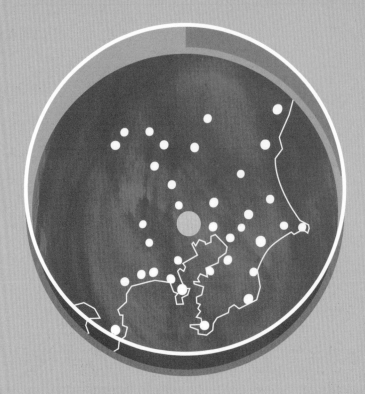

Start: Nakagaki and his team put a dollop of slime mould in a dish containing oat flakes. Slime mould likes to eat oats. The oat flakes were positioned where the most visited sites in Tokyo would appear on a map.

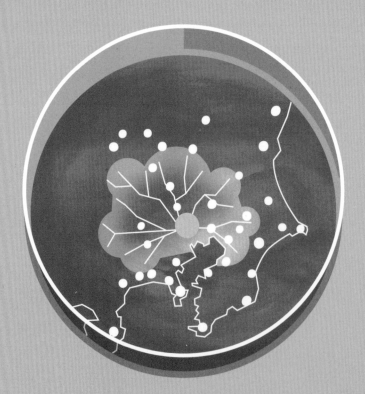

8 hours: The slime mould spread out all across the dish, looking for food.

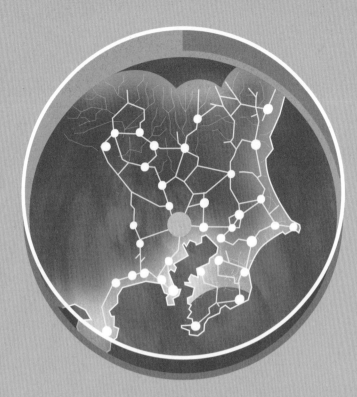

16 hours: The slime mould found the shortest route from one oat flake to another and shared that news through the whole blob.

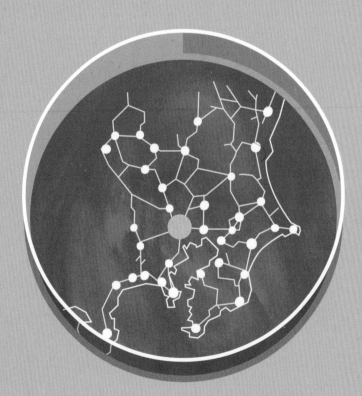

26 hours: The slime mould looked almost exactly like the Tokyo subway system. It found the easiest routes to the oat flakes, in the same way that the subway system is designed to transport people between city locations in the easiest way possible.

A common octopus named Inky lived at an aquarium in New Zealand. Octopuses have no bones, so they can can fit through super-small openings. One night Inky puzzled out how to escape. He squeezed himself through a 49-metre-long drainage pipe that went from his aquarium home straight out to the ocean. Octopuses are incredibly smart. Maybe Inky wanted to explore and ended up finding a new home in the sea.

INTELLIGENCE

INVENTION

Brooms, whisks and hammers ... drills, spoons and spanners. Tools make humans' lives easier. They extend our bodies, allowing our hands and feet to do things that would simply be impossible without them. For many years scientists thought only humans were capable of inventing tools. Then along came Jane Goodall.

Goodall is an English animal-lover and scientist who has studied chimpanzees for more than fifty-five years. She is now the world's leading expert on how they behave. Her most remarkable discovery was that chimps, like us, invent and use tools. In 1960, she began her research at Gombe Stream National Park in Tanzania. She stayed in a tent right near a group of chimpanzees. That way she could watch them all day and all night long. She got to know them as individuals and called them by names. What she discovered changed the way we think about animals (and humans) forever.

Before Jane Goodall, scientists looked at animals as species, trying to learn what the group had in common. But Goodall hadn't been trained in scientific research, so she watched the chimps in her own way, just as if she were watching people. In doing so, she invented a whole new way of studying animals. Her method is used by many scientists today.

Chimpanzees use tools to help with many tasks. They scratch their itchy backs with sticks. They make sponges out of mashed leaves and use them to soak up water for drinking. They have even been seen using large sticks to beat a bees' nest. Then, when the nest breaks, they use smaller twigs to spoon out the honey inside to eat as a sweet treat.

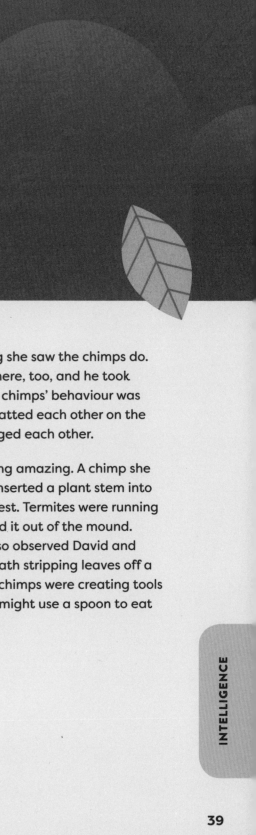

Goodall wrote down everything she saw the chimps do. A photographer came to live there, too, and he took pictures. It turned out that the chimps' behaviour was very much like humans'. They patted each other on the back, and they kissed and hugged each other.

One day, Goodall saw something amazing. A chimp she had named David Greybeard inserted a plant stem into an air hole in a giant termite nest. Termites were running all over the stick when he pulled it out of the mound. What a delicious snack! She also observed David and another chimp she named Goliath stripping leaves off a twig. It became clear that the chimps were creating tools to help them eat – just like we might use a spoon to eat our breakfast porridge!

It's not just chimps who use tools. In Australia, black kites use a very dramatic one. They carry burning sticks from forest fires to nearby grasslands and drop them to start fires in the grass. Why on earth would they do this? The answer is that it's a super clever form of hunting. As reptiles, insects and small mammals flee the burning grass, the kites swoop down and munch them for lunch.

Sea creatures get into the act, too. Bottlenose dolphins that live in Shark Bay in Western Australia have been seen wearing sea sponges over their beaks while hunting. It's thought that the dolphins use the sponges to protect their beaks from shards of coral and rocks on the sea-floor.

Moving Cars as Tools for Crows

What's the best way to crack a nut if you're a nut-loving crow? Well in Japan some crows seem to have figured out how to use humans as tools. It all started when some city crows dropped nuts onto a road, hoping the hard fall onto pavement would crack them. Then other crows improved on the system. They perch by pedestrian crossings, drop their nuts into the traffic so cars run over them, then wait for the light to turn red so they can swoop down and collect the nuts from the broken shells.

Some scientists think the crows are doing it on purpose. Others are not so sure. But that's how science works. Scientists make an observation and develop a hypothesis (a guess based on evidence) about it. Then they or others test the hypothesis to figure out whether it's true. Are these crows using moving cars as tools? The jury is still out.

In fact, the jury is still out for many animal behaviours. Just think ... what other creatures could be humanimal?

Researchers believe that corvids, a bird family including crows, ravens and rooks, are intelligent in similar ways to apes and humans. They are flexible, use imagination, think about the future, and know that a cause leads to an effect.

GLOSSARY

Behavioural ecologist
Someone who studies how humans or animals behave within their communities.

Biologist
A scientist who works on living things like animals and plants.

Climate change
Process in which environmental conditions on Earth change over time.

Cortisol
A type of chemical released by the body to help deal with stress or danger.

Deception
The act of tricking, lying or fibbing.

Dopamine
A type of chemical released by the body that makes you feel happy.

Ecologist
Someone who studies the relationship between living things and their environment.

Ethologist
Someone who studies animal behaviour.

Field station
A temporary home for researchers while observing animals in the wild.

Fungus
Organism that feeds on living or once-living things and reproduces using spores.

Hypothesis
A guess based on evidence, which is then tested by scientists to work out whether it is true.

Indigenous
Original, for example the first people who lived in a particular place, or their descendants.

Insect
Arthropod with six legs, three body parts and usually wings as well, such as a beetle.

Intelligence
The ability to learn things and develop skills.

Mammal
An animal with a backbone, which produces milk and, usually, gives birth to live young.

Marine biologist
Someone who studies living things in the sea.

Mutualism
When two living things are dependant on one another for their survival.

Naturalist
Someone who studies nature.

Predator
An animal that hunts another animal for food.

Psychologist
Someone who studies the mind.

Researcher
Someone who carries out research to understand something better.

Self-awareness
The act of knowing who you are and what you are like as a character.

Vocalisation
Expressing yourself using words or sounds.

Zoologist
A scientist who studies animals.

STUDYING ANIMALS

Ecologists, ethologists, marine biologists, psychologists, zoologists ...
there are many types of scientists who study how animals behave.
As you've seen, there are different ways they make new discoveries –
from living with chimps in the wild to observing slime mould in a petri
dish. Here's more information about the scientists in this book.

Andrew Adamatzky
Andrew Adamatzky is a computer scientist
at the University of the West of England,
Bristol. As well as observing slime mould, he
researches robotics. He enjoys spending time
with his dog, who he never talks to because
they understand each other in silence.

Anne Innis Dagg
Anne Innis Dagg first met giraffes at a zoo
when she was three years old, and has loved
them ever since. Aged twenty-three, she
went to Africa on her own to study giraffes
in the wild. She went on to become professor
of women's studies at the University of
Waterloo, Ontario, Canada.

Gail Damerow
Gail Damerow lives in Tennessee, USA, with
her husband, where they run a family farm
with chickens and dairy goats, a garden
and a small orchard. She has written about
chickens, other animals and rural life in more
than a dozen books as well as magazines.

Anne Engh
Anne Engh is the laboratory coordinator at Kalamazoo College in Michigan, USA. She spent two years living in a tent in a national park studying baboons. She had a few heart-pounding encounters – she was lifted up in a boat by a hippo and chased by elephants!

Karl von Frisch
Karl von Frisch was a Nobel Prize-winning Austrian ethologist. He did pioneering research on honeybees, along with Martin Lindauer, who was a German behavioural scientist.

Gordon G. Gallup, Jr.
Gordon G. Gallup, Jr. is an evolutionary psychologist at the University at Albany – SUNY in New York State, USA. As well as his work on how primates can recognise themselves in a mirror, he has studied the relationships between predators and prey and why the dinosaurs went extinct.

Shifra Goldenberg
Shifra Goldenberg is a behavioural ecologist at Smithsonian Conservation Biology Institute. She has a passion for studying animal behaviour to better understand threatened and endangered species. She is especially fond of pachyderms (mammals with thick skin, such as elephants).

Jane Goodall
Jane Goodall went to Tanzania in Africa to study chimpanzees in the wild when she was twenty-six. Her discovery that chimps use tools rocked the scientific world. She went on to gain a PhD in ethology from Cambridge University and establish the Jane Goodall Institute to build on her pioneering work.

Hiroki Hata
Hiroki Hata is an assistant professor in the biology department at Ehime University in Japan. His interests include the habitat, diet and behaviour of fish. As well as dusky farmerfish, he has studied coral communities and endangered species.

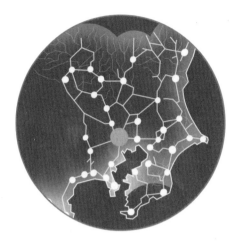

Toshiyuki Nakagaki
Toshiyuki Nakagaki is a professor of mathematical and physical ethology at Hokkaido University in Japan. He has conducted many research studies on slime mould, including how it makes decisions and travels around objects.

Cláudia Oliveira
Cláudia Oliveira is a marine biologist at the Institute of Marine Research in the Azores, a group of Portuguese islands in the Atlantic Ocean. Her interests include the bioacoustics of marine mammals and behavioural ecology.

Irene Pepperberg
Irene Pepperberg is is a research associate in the psychology department at Harvard University in Massachusetts, USA. Her research on a grey parrot called Alex changed the way people thought about bird intelligence. Before Alex died in 2007, his last words were for Irene, 'You be good. I love you.'

Joshua Plotnik
Joshua Plotnik is a comparative psychologist and conservation behaviour researcher at Hunter College, the City University of New York. Studying elephants in Thailand, he discovered that just like us, elephants have different personalities, and no two are alike.

David Scheel
David Scheel is a professor of marine biology at Alaska Pacific University. He lived alongside lions and wild dogs in Africa, and has found octopuses living close together in a community off the coast of Australia. He loves diving and photographing wildlife.

Magnus Wahlberg
Magnus Wahlberg leads the Marine Biological Research Center, which is the field station of the University of Southern Denmark. He is mainly interested in hearing and sound production of marine mammals and birds.

INDEX

SELECTED SOURCES

Adamatzky, Andrew and Jeff Jones, 2009. 'Road planning with slime mould: If *Physarum* built motorways it would route M6/M74 through Newcastle.' *Arxiv*.

Anderson, D.J. and R.E. Ricklefs, 1995. 'Evidence of Kin-Selected Tolerance by Nestlings in a Siblicidal Bird.' *Behavioral Ecology and Sociobiology*.

Bekoff, Marc, 2008. *The Emotional Lives of Animals: A Leading Scientist Explores Animal Joy, Sorrow, and Empathy—and Why They Matter*. Novato, California: New World Library.

Bonta, Mark, 2017. 'Intentional Fire-Spreading by "Firehawk" Raptors in Northern Australia.' *Journal of Ethnobiology*.

Collias, Nicholas, 1987. 'The Vocal Repertoire of the Red Junglefowl: A Spectrographic Classification and the Code of Communication.' *The Condor*.

Dagg, Anne Innis, 2014. *Giraffe Biology, Behaviour and Conservation*. Cambridge, Cambridge University Press.

Damerow, Gail, 2012. *The Chicken Encyclopedia: An Illustrated Reference*. North Adams, Massachusetts: Storey Publishing.

Diamond, Jared, 1986. 'Animal art: Variation in bower decorating style among male bowerbirds *Amblyornis inornatus*.' *Proceedings of the National Academy of Sciences*.

Engh, Anne, 2006. 'Behavioural and hormonal responses to predation in female chacma baboons (*Papio hamadryas ursinus*).' *Proceedings of the Royal Society B*.

Flower, Tom, et al., 2014. 'Deception by Flexible Alarm Mimicry in an African Bird.' *Science*.

Gallup, Gordon Jr., 1970. 'Chimpanzees: self-recognition.' *Science*.

Goodall, Jane, 1986. *The Chimpanzees of Gombe*. Boston: Belknap Press.

Hata, Hiroki and Makoto Kato, 2002. 'Weeding by the herbivorous damselfish *Stegastes nigricans* in nearly monocultural algae farms.' *Marine Ecology Progress Series*.

Huffard, Christine, et al., 2010. 'The evolution of conspicuous facultative mimicry in octopuses: an example of secondary adaptation?' *Biological Journal of the Linnean Society*.

Miller, Peter, 2010. *The Smart Swarm*. New York: Penguin.

Morell, Virginia, 2013. *Animal Wise: How We Know Animals Think and Feel*. New York: Broadway Books.

Nihei, Yoshiaki and Hiroyoshi Higuchi, 2001. 'When and where did crows learn to use automobiles as nutcrackers.' *Tohoku Psychologica Folia*.

Nygaard, Sanne, et al., 2016. 'Reciprocal genomic evolution in the ant–fungus agricultural symbiosis.' *Nature Communications*.

Oliveira, Cláudia, et al., 2016. 'Sperm whale codas may encode individuality as well as clan identity.' *The Journal of the Acoustical Society of America*.

Pepperberg, Irene, 2002. *The Alex Studies: Cognitive and Communicative Abilities of Grey Parrots*. Boston: Harvard University Press.

Plotnik, Joshua, et al., 2006. 'Self-recognition in an Asian elephant.' *Proceedings of the National Academy of Sciences*.

Tan, Jingzhi and Brian Hare, 2013. 'Bonobos Share with Strangers.' *PLOS One*.

Tero, Atsushi, et al., 2010. 'Rules for Biologically Inspired Adaptive Network Design.' *Science*.

Turner, J. Scott, 2000. 'Architecture and morphogenesis in the mound of *Macrotermes michaelseni* (Sjöstedt) (Isoptera: Termitidae, Macrotermitinae) in northern Namibia.' *Cimbebasia*.

Turner, J. Scott and Rupert C. Soar, 2008. 'Beyond biomimicry: What termites can tell us about realizing the living building.' First International Conference on Industrialized, Intelligent Construction.

Von Frisch, Karl and Martin Lindauer, 1956. 'The "Language" and Orientation of the Honey Bee.' *Annual Review of Entomology*.

ACKNOWLEDGEMENTS

It has been such a joy to write this little book that touches on one of the biggest questions in all reality. In truth, its creation has been very humanimal – a product of genuine teamwork. I am blessed with the most wonderful colleagues at What on Earth Publishing, in particular Ali Glossop (Editor), Assunção Sampayo (Designer) and Andy Forshaw (Art Director) who have all made enormous contributions to this book. Thanks to Mark Ruffle for his brilliant illustrations and to Michelle Harris for her tireless research. Thanks also to Lisa Morris, Grace Hill Smith and Carron Brown for their editorial rigour. Even more special thanks go to our publisher and editor-in-chief Nancy Feresten, whose idea this really was and whose genius fingerprints are imprinted on every page.

What on Earth Books is an imprint of What on Earth Publishing
The Black Barn, Wickhurst Farm, Tonbridge, Kent TN11 8PS, United Kingdom
30 Ridge Road Unit B, Greenbelt, Maryland, 20770, United States

First published in the United Kingdom in 2019

Staff for this book: Ali Glossop, Editor; Assunção Sampayo, Designer;
Andy Forshaw, Art Director

Research consultant: Michelle Harris

A CIP catalogue record for this book is available from the British Library

ISBN: 978-1-912920-00-6

Printed in China

10 9 8 7 6 5 4 3 2 1

MIX
Paper from
responsible sources
FSC® C137129

whatonearthbooks.com